It's A Rap!

Rhythm And Poetry for Teens & Young Adults

Written & Illustrated by
Judy M. Jackson & Amanda J. Jackson

Published by
For His Glory Publications

All scripture quotations are taken from the *Holy Bible*, *King
James Version* (KJV).

Published by For His Glory Publications
P.O. Box 911
Clinton, MD 20735

To order via website: www.fhgpublications.com
or,
Write us at the above address or e-mail us at:
fhgpublications@hotmail.com

Authors' Photo by Michael L. Jackson

Drawing on cover & chapter title pages done by
Vincent Lockett

05-1230
FOR HIS GLORY PR
(AMAZON)
11/05
$9.95

This book is presented to:

_____

_____

From:

_____

_____

On the occasion of:

_____

_____

Date:

_____

Please do not read the personal journal entries without the permission of the owner named above.

CONTENTS

I. Young Ladies

II. Young Men

III. Young Ladies & Young Men

IV. Resources

FOREWORD

By Catherine B. Curtis
First Lady, Christ's Church, Waldorf, MD
Co-author, "The Fine Art of Marriage:
When Two Become One"

This Godly compilation of poetry by a mother and answered by her daughter, coupled with scripture reading, is a very enriching work to read. Written to both young ladies and young men for this present day and beyond, it is very inspiring and insightful into the daily occurrences that face our children. Making wise decisions now can prevent a lifetime of heartache and misery. The very fact that they have taken the time to put their learning experiences in a book for others to read and gain more wisdom, shows the love of God being passed on for generations to come. Those who read and receive instructions will gain more wisdom from what is being shared in this publication; and they can avoid the pitfalls, dangers and snares that may await them without this Godly knowledge.

In this time in which we are living, so many young lives have been sacrificed in the streets. Our youth of today face different pressures than what their parents faced. Trying to make it through school and graduate is a challenge by itself. We have seen and continue to see and hear the explosions going on in the schools. Yet we must still live in this world, work, do business and guide our affairs, taking advantage of every opportunity given in these walls. We cannot hide in our homes. Godly instructions proceeding from the homes, as we go forth to learn and do, will be what keep us safe.

I applaud mother and daughter in their efforts to see this excellent work brought to fruition. May God continue to bless, enrich, and tighten your bond together as you labor in sharing from the heart those life lessons that you have learned and now are willing to lovingly share so others can be blessed, edified, and built up in the most holy faith.

REVIEW

By Donald B. Curtis
Pastor, Christ's Church, Waldorf, MD
Co-author, "The Fine Art of Marriage:
When Two Become One"

This is a unique mother-daughter teamwork, as they reflect on some very important issues today's teens face. They speak to both young men and young women. The mother uses poems to express issues she knows teens and young adults are dealing with today, keeping in mind her own daughter and son. To add to that, her daughter writing as "Mandi's Minute" provides a young teen's view and follow-up of the issues raised by the poem. Mandi's Minute also provides some insightful encouragement and challenges to the reader.

This work is user friendly. It has probing questions, space to write down your thoughts, and personal insights by the issues raised throughout. It is meant to be personal. There is, in it's beginning, a request to only read the written contents with the owner's approval. You can carry this with you wherever, and make it a personal place to journal some of your personal thoughts. Because of it's personal nature, you may not want to share the contents of this work with others, but you will want to encourage them to get a copy for themselves and their personal notes.

Take your time and read through each section. Slow down and think through the messages they contain. Reflect on them. Give them time to open up to you issues that may be in your heart that, once resolved, can unlock a new and fresh world of spiritual freedom.

DEDICATIONS

This book is dedicated first to God – thank you for instilling in me a desire to write and encourage your children. It is also dedicated to my husband, Michael L. Jackson. It was in the planning of Mike's 40th birthday party that God brought forth my gift of poetry. I wrote my first poem as a tribute to my husband. I love you very much honey!

To my children, Amanda J. Jackson & Phillip M. Jackson: You are my precious gems, and I thank God for you daily.

To my siblings, Essie Johnson, Stephen Mikell, Levester Mikell, Loreatha Slater, Dorothy Clifton, Johnny Slater & Willie Slater: We are together forever! Much love to my stepsiblings and all of my beloved family.

To my mother-in-law, Pauline Jackson: Thanks for the many years of sacrificing to assist us. We love you Mom! To Vincent, Charmain, Kelly & Shakira Jackson: Keep moving forward in love!

In loving memory of:
- Levester Mikell, Sr., My dad
- Emma Mikell, My mom
- Bernice Mikell, My stepmom
- Essie M. Mikell, My grandmom
- James Mikell, My brother
- Rev. James H. Neal, Pastor, Mt. Ennon Baptist Church (My first Pastor as a Christian adult)

ACKNOWLEDGEMENTS

We wish to thank the many people who have assisted in the writing of this book in any way. Thanks to Darlene M. Claiborne, Acts of Kindness Ministries, for your proofreading and editorial comments. Your assistance is truly an act of kindness. Thanks to our Pastor (Donald B. Curtis), First Lady (Catherine B. Curtis), leaders, and the Christ's Church family for your many prayers; and a special thank-you to Pastor Curtis for encouraging me to read my first poem – a tribute to my husband – amidst the entire congregation.

Much love and appreciation to my former First Lady, Minister Rhonda L. Neal, Mt. Ennon Baptist Church, Clinton, MD for the love, guidance, and encouragement that you and your husband, the late Rev. James H. Neal, have shown to my family and I during the nine years that we were under your ministry.

Much gratitude to the many people at work who have encouraged me to write; and to the *CFIRE* Christian organization, Bible study, and prayer group at work.

ABOUT THE AUTHORS

The authors are a mother-daughter team who share many of the same talents.   They have shared many activities together including: piano lessons, art lessons, and now they share their love for creative writing together.

Amanda is on the Praise Dance Ministry, and is Vice President of our church Youth Ministry. In her spare time, Amanda enjoys designing hair-braiding styles.

Judy has been involved in youth ministry throughout her Christian walk. She is the mother of two teens, and has always enjoyed being involved in their lives, as well as in the lives of their friends and our relatives. She tries to use every opportunity to "pour wisdom" into their lives.

They both have drawn on their experiences, and the realization of the world in which we live for inspiration for this book.

I. Young Ladies

Beware

(1 John 2:15-16)

Beware of the wolves who roam among the flock,
We were warned of them by
Jesus Christ, the Solid Rock!

You've seen 'em –
they hang outside high schools,

saying "girl, you don't need to date them
high school boys, hang out with me …
I'll show you things you never would see."

Recognize it – It's not God's voice.

What they can show,
you don't want to see …

Like the inside of prison walls,
being detained,
unable to be free!

They think they're all that,
But they're not!

Always flaunting their money …
Telling you … "Let me show you what I got."

I had one tell me, "if you be my girl,
I'll buy you a diamond ring" –

Appealing to the eyes …
They think young ladies like to "bling-bling!"

They watch you and know you like to dress …

Had the nerve to say "sleep with me &
I'll buy you Gucci, Louis & Guess"

Child of God, you better get bold & wise …

Tell 'em, you don't need a gem –
You are a gem – not a cheap bubblegum prize!

They obviously, can't possibly know,
Your Father owns the world; He runs the show.

How dare they approach you like
you're some enterprising whore

Stay with God, and if He desires,
you won't just have the merchandise,
you'll own the entire store!

And, … if they can give you so much,
Why aren't they at work?

Instead of grown men
hanging out at high school basketball courts.

Brother, get a job & someone your own age.

Here's a thought …
Go give General Motors or General Electric a page …

Talk to Jesus, He's got what you need;
Stop messin' up young people's lives

Pray; and even pick up the Bible & read.

Mandi's
Minute

Hold up, wait a minute, let Amanda get up in it!

"Ladies, if you feel me, stand up! Look ya'll, I know we like money, jewelry, clothes, and accessories—all that; but we can't be used for it. It's not right, and definitely not of God. We have to take a stand and say no, I have more respect for myself than to let someone walk all over me. Most importantly, without esteem for ourselves, how can we have it for the Most High God? He's the one who deserves your time of day! Oh yeah, and ladies if you've been the user, stop being a straight up gold-digger and get a J.O.B.! Holla"

*****

Biblical Scripture

1 John 2:15-16 (KJV):

Love not the world, neither the things that are in the world. If any man love the world, the love of the Father is not in him.

For all that is in the world, the lust of the flesh, and the lust of the eyes, and the pride of life, is not of the Father, but is of the world.

Reflections

1. Has anyone ever offered to buy you things in exchange for sex? If so, what was your reaction?

_____

_____

_____

_____

_____

_____

_____

2. One way to avoid being tempted to accept gifts from others is to be content with the things that you have. If you are old enough to work, get a summer job and establish your own savings account. List other responsible ways of saving money.

_____

_____

_____

_____

_____

_____

_____

Think It Not Strange

(1 Peter 4:12-13)

Daughters, I know where you are!
The difficulties you encounter
Seems as though no one understands
Trying to find your place in life … To fit in?

Think it not strange my sistas
When you feel like an outsider!
You have been set apart; sanctified …
To bring glory to your Father!

So, my daughters … think it not strange
When so-called friends try to draw you
into their craziness.
Don't give in!

Don't give in to the offers of sex –
no matter how cute or smooth-talking he is!
It's a trap – designed to take you off course.

No! Don't give in.
Don't give in to the offers of lesbianism –
they present it as if it's the in thing! Don't give in!

Say no to the devil's devices!
Say no to those who promote his schemes!
His plan is simple:
To stop you even before you know your purpose.
To stop you even before you begin to dream.
That's why so much is presented to you –
yes, while you're still in high school.

Don't they know that you are
children of the Most High God?

You know your purpose,
you know God's plan.
You keep His Words in your mouth day and night.
Meditate on it!
And your Father makes your way prosperous
and causes you to have good success –
success in school,
success with your parents,
success in every area of your life.

Don't abort or stop the dream!

Choose God in your daily life;
Choose peace and avoid strife!

And, think it not strange when your Heavenly Father
does the miraculous in your life.

It's your destiny my daughters!
So, think it not strange!

Mandi's Minute

Hold up, wait a minute, let Amanda get up in it!

"True, true, there's always a question in the back of my mind, like 'how do you know this?' Well, to back up this answer, you read the Word of God. He'll never steer you wrong. See ya!"

*****

Biblical Scripture

1 Peter 4:12-13 (KJV):

Beloved, think it not strange concerning the fiery trial which is to try you, as though some strange thing happened unto you:

But rejoice, inasmuch as ye are partakers of Christ's sufferings; that, when his glory shall be revealed, ye may be glad also with exceeding joy.

Think About It ...

Don't be surprised or perplexed when people approach you with crazy ideas or try to get you to do things that you know are wrong.

Again, don't be surprised – just do what you know is right and pray for God to keep you from evil. He will!

18

Reflections

1. Has anyone approached you with crazy ideas or tried to get you to participate in things that you knew were wrong (e.g., lesbianism, etc.)? If so, please explain.

   _____

   _____

   _____

   _____

   _____

   _____

2. What was your reaction?

   _____

   _____

   _____

   _____

   _____

   _____

3. After reading the aforementioned scripture, identify how you could handle the situation differently if approached again.

   _____

   _____

   _____

   _____

   _____

Learn To Walk Alone

(Matthew 7:13-14)

Do you yearn for friends who understand your plight,
who will tell you you're wrong,
even when you think you're right?

Just when you think a true friend you've found,
it turns out she's just like the others,
lots of drama to be around!

So you go through life looking,
searching for a friend who is similar to you.
Until one day you realize, wake up and it hits you – BOOM!
God wants you to just be you –
stop perpetrating, trying to fit in, just be you!

Around 10th grade in high school,
God made me comfortable with being me.
No more seeking, never seeming to find …
Even if everyone turned their backs on me,
treated me unkind …
It doesn't matter when you are comfortable with yourself …

Let God add the friendships –
since He knows their hearts …

Let Him subtract – those to be kept apart …
From you … those who would seek to stop His mission for
your life …

Learn to walk alone!
Learn to walk alone!

You're never alone when you walk with Jesus!

Drawing by Amanda J. Jackson

Mandi's
Minute

Hold up, wait a minute, let Amanda get up in it!

"Let me tell ya'll something, you're never alone when you're walking with Jesus. Avoid peer pressure by being comfortable with yourself; and know that God is always with you. You can have all the friends in the world, but no one could compare to the love of Jesus Christ. He's my best friend! Have a closer walk with Him!"

*****

Biblical Scripture

Matthew 7:13-14 (KJV):

Enter ye in at the strait gate: for wide is the gate, and broad is the way, that leadeth to destruction, and many there be which go in thereat:

Because strait is the gate, and narrow is the way, which leadeth unto life, and few there be that find it.

Reflections

1. Were there times in your life when you were tempted to go with the crowd just to fit in and be accepted? If so, please explain.

_____

_____

_____

_____

_____

_____

_____

2. The preceding scripture illustrates that it is not good to follow the crowd. You should do what you know is right and pray for God's guidance. List some practical ways to be led by God.

_____

_____

_____

_____

_____

_____

_____

II. Young Men

Love of Money

(1 Timothy 6:10-11)

Guys, don't be tempted by the fast dollar

Don't listen to drug dealers and criminals
Saying, "come here, let me give you a holler".

And, don't hang out with drug users –
marijuana, cocaine, crack & alcohol abusers;

The drugs keep them paralyzed;
Their dreams may never be realized.

Think about what got them there,
… Lack of enthusiasm,
… Gave up on life, or
… They just didn't care.

10 years from now, where will you be?
… In that successful career?
Or on the corner smokin' weed & drinkin' beer?

Decisions …
Choices …
Maybe I'll get to it
Stop procrastinating
[actin' like it's so hard]
And makin' excuses –
Just do it!

Be willing to work hard,
even volunteer your time ...
Listen to your conscious,
... your sublime

Before you do anything,
Consider the possible outcome

Ask yourself: Is this a path I should take
or should I shun?

... the activity

And ask God to lead you to your destiny

In the meantime, avoid idleness &
passivity!

Mandi's Minute

Hold up, wait a minute, let Amanda get up in it!

"I know it's challenging being a Christian teen in the world today (I'm struggling myself), but the Lord is able to give us strength and dedication to fight the temptations!"

*****

Biblical Scripture

I Timothy 6:10-11 (KJV):

For the love of money is the root of all evil: which while some coveted after, they have erred from the faith, and pierced themselves through with many sorrows.

But thou, O man of God, flee these things; and follow after righteousness, godliness, faith, love, patience, meekness.

Reflections

1. God's strength is able to keep us from falling. However, we must apply His principles to our lives in order to be victorious. List some ways you can avoid the traps of the enemy.

_____

_____

_____

_____

_____

_____

_____

2. Read the aforementioned scripture and identify the thing that causes us to turn away from God.

_____

_____

_____

_____

_____

_____

_____

Similitude

(Leviticus 18:22)

Sameness

God says abstinence – no sex at all
until the day
He brings the virgin your way
To be your bride.

Prayerfully, she'll be someone trained,
reared up and taught to appreciate you,
and your decision to say no
until the day you both say "I do."

And what about this trend
Young men with young men …

Similitude …

Denounce it!

Don't pray for good grades only,
Pray also that God will satisfy your true desires
And keep you from feeling lonely.

He'll comfort your heart
And your disappointment,

Endow you with power
… and His anointment.

Mandi's
Minute

Hold up, wait a minute, let Amanda get up in it!

"Whoa, that's a lot to take in, but yet so true. What does our Father have to say?" ...

*****

Biblical Scripture

Leviticus 18:22 (KJV):

Thou shalt not lie with mankind, as with womankind: it is abomination [sin].*

* Word in brackets was added by author for clarity.

Reflections

1. Has anyone approached you to have a homosexual relationship? If so, what was your reaction?

_____

_____

_____

_____

_____

_____

2. Read the scripture on the preceding page and write down what God is saying to you in this scripture.

_____

_____

_____

_____

_____

_____

Your Girl Will Be A Queen

(Esther 2:9)

Your girl will be a queen,

What do I mean?

Like Queen Esther, she'll be purified

Been taught in poise, temperance, respect, honor

… taught how to give a gentle answer, encourage

… Know how to receive

She'll know how to seek God – communicate,

She'll even know how to respect you while out on a date.

And, of course, you've gone through a similar type of grooming

So when the Lord decides,

You'll know how to treat her
When you make her your bride.

Mandi's Minute

Hold up, wait a minute, let Amanda get up in it!

"Personally (from a girl's perspective), I've been single/free for a minute, but it doesn't bother me. I'm not rushing anything, nor looking for a boyfriend. I'm just enjoying having good friends. I know in God's time, he'll come for me; and, when he comes, he'll know how to treat me & I'll be prepared for him. So, as of now, I'm just living life to the fullest and having fun along the way."

*****

Biblical Scripture

Esther 2:9 (KJV):

And the maiden pleased him, and she obtained kindness of him; and he speedily gave her her things for purification, with such things as belonged to her, and seven maidens, which were meet [proper] to be given her, out of the king's house: and he preferred her and her maids unto the best place of the house of the women.*

* Word in brackets was added by author for clarity.

Reflections

1. What are the characteristics you look for in a girlfriend?

_____

_____

_____

_____

_____

_____

_____

2. After reflecting on God's Word, write down the qualities you believe God would have you seek in a girlfriend.

_____

_____

_____

_____

_____

_____

_____

III. Young Ladies & Young Men

Chastity

(Luke 1:27; Matthew 1:24-25)

So, you've taken a vow of chastity –
Remain chaste – a virgin until married.

Then satan sends someone to tempt you who says
"you can abstain from intercourse,
but have oral sex instead" –
Don't let the enemy plant lies in your head!

Just like the serpent beguiled Eve,
Learn a lesson and don't you be deceived.

Any kind of sex without being married is not in God's plan

Sex was designed for intimacy in marriage –
Between a woman and her man!

This is just a warning,
whenever you make a vow

The deceiver is always nearby to throw darts at you,
but his plan of deception we won't allow!

Ask God for wisdom and then utilize,
To avoid situations that might yield compromise.

You've got the power to abstain,
In Jesus' name!

Mandi's Minute

Hold up, wait a minute, let Amanda get up in it!

"To me, being a virgin is very sacred. The reason for that is when you fornicate with someone you create a soul tie. So, when you decide to marry your husband or wife, you might not be able to focus on your marriage as you should because of flashbacks to past sexual relationships. Abstaining might seem difficult now, but explore the scriptures to avoid future complications."

*****

Biblical Scriptures

Luke 1:27 (KJV):

To a virgin espoused to a man whose name was Joseph, of the house of David; and the virgin's name was Mary.

Matthew 1:24-25 (KJV):

Then Joseph being raised from sleep did as the angel of the Lord had bidden him, and took unto him his wife:

And knew her not [did not have sex with her*] till she had brought forth her firstborn son: and he called his name JESUS.

* Words in brackets were added by author for clarity.

Think About It ...

If God had decided to wait 'til now to send our Savior, Jesus Christ, into the world, I wonder if He would have had a difficult time finding a virgin?

Even though our Lord and Savior, Jesus Christ, has already come, I believe God still has some awesome plans for your life; and He still desires virgins.

Why don't you decide to be that remnant for God to use?

Reflections

1. Have you had temptation to be sexually active? If so, please explain.

_____

_____

_____

_____

_____

_____

_____

_____

2. List some ways you can avoid being caught in a compromising situation (e.g., double dating with a close friend who shares your values; date only people with a reputation for being respectful; invite your date to your house to play family games, laugh and talk as a group).

_____

_____

_____

_____

_____

_____

_____

_____

Please Forgive Us

... A plea from parents to our young ladies & gentlemen

(Mark 11:25-26)

Please forgive us for being so harsh
We were only trying to protect you.

Please forgive us for accusing you
When things didn't seem to line up.

Please forgive us for comparing you
To your sister… your brother…

We may have been the culprit –
Causing you to compete against each other!

I apologize for parents everywhere …

We try to protect you,
But sometimes cause you to fall into a snare.

Pray for us, just as we pray for you.

We, too, have to seek God because
we're still learning and growing spiritually –
We don't always know what to do!

Please forgive us!

Mandi's
Minute

Hold up, wait a minute, let Amanda get up in it!

"I especially enjoy how my mom apologized for all the parents' mistakes they may have committed in the past. She kind of gave us a brief point of their view. I'm willing to forgive and forget because I know God does every time we sin; we repent, God forgives us, and life goes on. So, who are we not to be able to forgive? Think about it."

*****

Biblical Scripture

Mark 11:25-26 (KJV):

And when ye stand praying, forgive, if ye have ought against any: that your Father also which is in heaven may forgive you your trespasses.

But if ye do not forgive, neither will your Father which is in heaven forgive your trespasses.

Reflections

1. Do you have unforgiveness in your heart towards your parents? If so, please explain.

_____

_____

_____

_____

_____

_____

_____

2. Perhaps your parents didn't do everything quite the way you thought they should have. If you honestly think about it, you may find that you haven't done everything perfectly either. It is the devil's desire for us to be defeated. Unforgiveness is one of his tools. Maybe now is the time to ask God to help you forgive your parents. You can't do it on your own, God must help you to let go of the hurt and move toward a victorious future with your parents.

   List ways to stay in harmony with your parents.

_____

_____

_____

_____

_____

_____

_____

_____

Remember to apologize with humility and gentleness. The tone in which you speak is just as important as the apology itself. Ask for their forgiveness and let go of any bad feelings you were holding in your heart towards them. Even if they do not accept your apology, you can be free of guilt because you have honored God by apologizing to them! Once you have done this, don't let anyone make you feel condemned again. Know in your heart that God is working everything out. Go forward with a renewed relationship with your parents!

The Exam

(2 Corinthians 2:14)

So you've got an upcoming exam

Today is the day

Will you just begin

Or pause first to pray?

Do all you can –

Study, prepare and review

Try to do your best

Then be confident of what God will do!

Immediately thereafter

Thank God for the expected "A".

He's sure to honor you

Because you honored Him with faith to pray!

**Mandi's
Minute**

Hold up, wait a minute, let Amanda get up in it!

"Hey, don't take my mom's word for it, see what the scriptures have to say. Holla!"

*****

Biblical Scripture

2 Corinthians 2:14 (KJV):

Now thanks be unto God, which always causeth us to triumph in Christ, and maketh manifest [known] the savour of his knowledge by us in every place.*

* Word in brackets was added by author for clarity.

Reflections

1. Do you have a difficult exam coming up?

_____

_____

_____

_____

_____

2. Write down your concerns and pray for God's guidance. Do your part by studying, and then trust God for his supernatural abilities.

_____

_____

_____

_____

_____

3. Have you had victories in subjects that once were challenging? If so, write your victories down and thank God for them. This will help encourage you in the future.

_____

_____

_____

_____

_____

No More Tears!

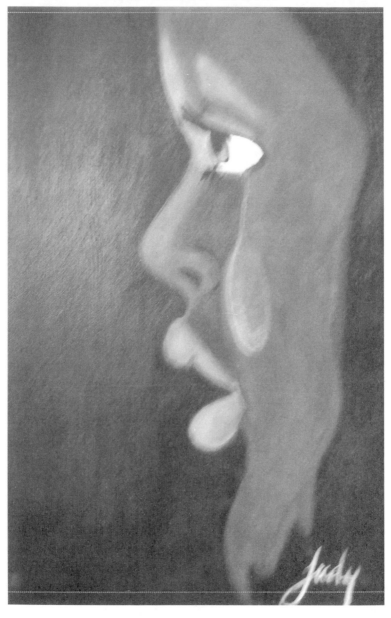

Painting by Judy M. Jackson

<u>No More Tears!</u>

(Isaiah 25:8)

No more tears!

I've cried long enough

Time to let go of that old, past stuff

Exchanged my frown for a hearty laugh

Learned to smile more,

Take things in stride,

Also laid down my silly pride!

I'm moving forward with finesse and tact,

Since my future is ahead of me, I won't look back!

Mandi's Minute

Hold up, wait a minute, let Amanda get up in it!

"If you ask me, I feel as though I'm tired of crying and 'No More Tears' is oh so true. Now I've grown wiser to know that all the trials that we're going through (as teens) are for a reason. Remember: We always have the victory – even if it might not seem like it, and our testimonies from these trials may even one day be a blessing for a person who is struggling or going through. Now, we can be the person that they can lean on for once."

*****

Biblical Scripture

Isaiah 25:8 (KJV):

He will swallow up death in victory; and the Lord GOD will wipe away tears from off all faces; and the rebuke of his people shall he take away from off all the earth: for the LORD hath spoken it.

Reflections

1. Have you been in a constant state of depression? If so, please explain.

_____

_____

_____

_____

_____

_____

2. It may be time to let go and let God! Allow God to heal you now. Use the space below to write down your concerns/troubles, then ask God to remove your burdens and thank him for doing just that.

_____

_____

_____

_____

_____

_____

3. Think positive thoughts to help lift your spirits. List some occasions or memories that immediately lift your spirits.

_____

_____

_____

_____

_____

_____

If you have depressing thoughts, think about happy occasions and the promises of a bright future that God has for those who love him. This will bring you gladness. Surround yourself with positive people who encourage you. Also, begin speaking God's promises for your life. See the "*biblical affirmations*" at the end of this book. These are a few of God's promises concerning you. Study the Bible and find more. Believe God to do positive things in your life.

<u>Be Selective</u>

(Psalms 1:1-3)

Be very selective about your friends
Find things in common
Before associating with them

Be sure to know
what they're into

Because who you
associate with

Becomes your
association too!

Seek wisdom from the wise,
Not counsel from fools

How can they lead you,
If they don't first follow the rules?

Mandi's
Minute

Hold up, wait a minute, let Amanda get up in it!

"You see, life is easier when you know right from wrong. Don't let nobody stop you from following Jesus Christ! Read God's scripture to back up the words of wisdom."

*****

Biblical Scriptures

Psalms 1:1-3 (KJV):

Blessed is the man that walketh not in the counsel of the ungodly, nor standeth in the way of sinners, nor sitteth in the seat of the scornful.

But his delight is in the law of the Lord; and in his law doth he meditate day and night.

And he shall be like a tree planted by the rivers of water, that bringeth forth his fruit in his season; his leaf also shall not wither; and whatsoever he doeth shall prosper.

Reflections

1. How well do you choose your friends? Write down some characteristics of your friends.

_____

_____

_____

_____

_____

_____

_____

_____

2. As you go through life, you will maintain contact with some of your friends for a lifetime. However, you may lose touch with others. Usually, those you keep in touch with will be the ones who are most like you and whose lifestyle is similar to yours.

   Which of your friends do you think are most likely to be in your life forever?

_____

_____

_____

_____

_____

_____

_____

_____

Love Covers!

(1 Peter 4:8)

Love covers a multitude of sin
We need it, as we all fall short now and then

Keep no record of wrong
Learn to pray about it, forgive, forget and move on.

Pray for your fellow man,
Even if his ways you don't understand

Prayer – It's a powerful tool you know
It helps to sustain us, enables us to grow!

Jesus gauges our discipleship by our love
As we abide in Him, getting guidance from above.

So cover your brothers … your sisters …
Don't let them go bare!

God wrapped His cloak of love around us
Gave us an example, showed us how to care.

Remember, love covers!

Mandi's Minute

Hold up, wait a minute, let Amanda get up in it!

"Let me tell ya'll, prayer works! If you're sincere, really want a change, and believe that you'll receive – the blessings will come down. Don't gossip about something you can't change. Just talking about it is useless. Show love by praying about the situation. God knows your heart. He sees all and knows all. Don't try to play Him, be straight up!"

*****

Biblical Scripture

1 Peter 4:8 (KJ V):

And above all things have fervent charity [love*] among yourselves: for charity [love*] shall cover the multitude of sins.

* Words in brackets were added by author for clarity.

Reflections

1. When someone has done you wrong, are you tempted to ruin their reputation by gossiping about them? If so, please explain.

_____

_____

_____

2. Next time someone does you wrong, try to peacefully discuss it with the person, if possible. Maybe they didn't intend to hurt you. Perhaps they didn't even know that you were offended. Either way, you should always pray about the situation and ask God to heal your heart so that unforgiveness does not set in.

   List some people you need to pray for and begin praying for them.

_____

_____

_____

_____

3. Keep a record of your answered prayers, and be sure to thank God for them.

_____

_____

_____

_____

Enjoy The Journey

(John 10:10)

Slow down,
Enjoy life
Take things in stride

While you're getting to your destiny
Take time to enjoy the ride

Keep balance:
Study, work
and play

Stop rushing through life
Learn also to rest and pray

Since we all must work,
Let's smile, be happy
And keep a sunny disposition

It helps us enjoy even
the most mundane job or position

~~~

Enjoy the journey while getting to your destiny!

~~~

Be happy doctors, lawyers, engineers, accountants,
entrepreneurs, and connoisseurs

Mandi's Minute

Hold up, wait a minute, let Amanda get up in it!

"Wow, some of these words I had to take a minute to sound out, but that's how we learn – by expanding our vocabulary. Let's see if any are in the Word of God."

★★★★★

Biblical Scripture

John 10:10 (KJV):

The thief cometh not, but for to steal, and to kill, and to destroy: I am come that they might have life, and that they might have it more abundantly.

Reflections

1. Do you dread going certain places, like school, work, or even church? If so, please explain.

_____

_____

_____

_____

_____

_____

_____

2. We all have responsibilities, but it doesn't have to be boring. You can make going to school, work, and church enjoyable by establishing friendships that may even last a lifetime. Stop complaining and start making friends! However, don't let the friends deter you from the real goal of being there.

   List some ways to improve your attitude about doing dreaded activities and/or chores.

_____

_____

_____

_____

_____

_____

_____

_____

It's Not As Bad As It Seems!

(Romans 8:28)

That situation that seems to be problematic
When kept in perspective, is not quite as bad as you had it
I'll say it again, I'll be emphatic...

When faced with issues that seem overwhelming

Take a day or two to stop, relax, and pray

Don't deal with it yet,
first try to get...
Rest to clear your mind,
Then seek advice – not just any kind,
but from people who have overcome in that way!

Live a life communicating with God
And the Holy Spirit will give you peace to settle issues that
once were frustrating and hard

~~~

On any given day,
Stop, rest and pray!

Mandi's
Minute

Hold up, wait a minute, let Amanda get up in it!

"You know, I've heard wise Christians tell me to give it up and let God take care of the rest. That means any struggles, hurt, or harm you've gone through – being able to step back, take a deep breath and let God. It might feel like you're down for the count, but you always have the victory with God. Just cry out to God in a sincere heart, and repent for your wrongs. Then just let God work, and please believe He's working behind the scenes. And, remember, God will never give you more than you can bear. See u on the flip side!"

*****

Biblical Scripture

Romans 8:28 (KJV):

And we know that all things work together for good to them that love God, to them who are the called according to his purpose.

Reflections

1. Are you facing a difficult situation? If so, please explain.

_____

_____

_____

_____

_____

_____

_____

2. Looking at the big picture might be overwhelming. So, just take it one step at a time. Don't make hasty decisions, but allow time for God to lead you.

   Also, involve your parents in your life's journey. You may be surprised to find out that those old folks have gone through similar issues as you. You may even have a laugh or two, as they tell you about how the enemy tried to trip them up. Who knows, the problem might be an opportunity for you and your parents to bond. God is awesome like that.

   List activities you can do with your parents and family members to foster a positive relationship.

_____

_____

_____

_____

_____

_____

_____

Why?

(Genesis 34:2-3)

There's all this talk about abstaining
But very few tell you why

They say, "don't have sex until married;
don't mess up like I"

But God still used them, they're ministering today;
So, why must I neglect having fun in the same way –
With this fly girl or fine guy?

I'm glad you asked, I'll tell you why!

You only see that we've turned out O.K.,
But what you don't see are the 20 years of mess
God had to strip away

He was our personal psychiatrist, therapist, exorcist too
Cast out demons! – Yes, more than a few!

Our minds go back sometimes, it seems like in a flash
Why did you get so upset when she only asked you to
"take out the trash?"

And she gets upset with him,
Thinks he's cheating, but he's just working out at the gym

All this sudden tension!!
From people in your past you forgot to mention.

Could it be those souls that clung to you –
Thoughts of that controlling babe or that cheating boo?

Perhaps these scenarios floating around in our heads are
manifestations of activities that went on in beds

God said man is to leave father and mother,
and cleave to his wife;
But fornication creates future strife

Seeds planted now will yield a future crop.
My advice is wait and don't bed hop!

Mandi's
Minute

Hold up, wait a minute, let Amanda get up in it!

"My brothers and sisters, I know it's hard to save yourselves until you're married, when the devil is right behind you putting thoughts in your head. Save your body (the temple for the Holy Spirit) and help others along the way. We can do it! Jesus is the way, the truth and the life. Let Him live in you. And, if the mistake of having sex before marriage was already made, don't give up hope; all you have to do is sincerely repent, and give up that sin that the devil THOUGHT he had you bound in! You're free in the name of Jesus."

*****

Biblical Scriptures

Genesis 34:2-3 (KJV):

And when Shechem the son of Hamor the Hivite, prince of the country, saw her, he took her, and lay with her, and defiled her.

And his soul clave [clung*] unto Dinah the daughter of Jacob, and he loved the damsel, and spake kindly unto the damsel.

* Word in brackets added by author for clarity.

Reflections

1. Can you think of any situations that are a direct result of fornication? If so, please list them.

_____

_____

_____

_____

_____

_____

_____

2. Our society faces many problems that can be traced back to fornication. Some of these include teenage pregnancy, abortion, sexually-transmitted diseases such as AIDS, etc. There are other struggles that families face as a result of fornication, such as all children not having the same father. This may create division in a future marriage.

   You may enhance your marriage relationship by avoiding fornication. List other reasons for waiting.

_____

_____

_____

_____

_____

_____

_____

There's Hope!

If you have found yourself on the pages of this book, either as a victim or as an offender, whatever the case may be, God wants you to know that there's hope!

You can be healed, set free, and delivered from sin's grip. However, you must do your part by confessing your sins, asking for God's forgiveness, and then seeking to obey God.

Biblical Scripture

1 John 1:9 (KJV):

If we confess our sins, he is faithful and just to forgive us our sins, and to cleanse us from all unrighteousness.

Now is a good time to repent, turn toward God, and receive a fresh start.

Prayer

Father God, please forgive me for the wrong that I've done. Please cleanse me from all unrighteousness, and give me a fresh start that I may serve you with gladness. Please lead me to Godly believers who will help me to grow in faith and love. In Jesus' name I pray. Amen.

IV.

Resources

Biblical Affirmations

John 14:23-24 –

Jesus answered and said unto him, If a man love me, he will keep my words: and my Father will love him, and we will come unto him, and make our abode with him.

He that loveth me not keepeth not my sayings: and the word which ye hear is not mine, but the Father's which sent me.

Hebrews 11:6 –

But without faith it is impossible to please him: for he that cometh to God must believe that he is, and that he is a rewarder of them that diligently seek him.

2 Timothy 1:7 –

For God hath not given us the spirit of fear; but of power, and of love, and of a sound mind.

Psalm 91:1 –

He that dwelleth in the secret place of the most High shall abide under the shadow of the Almighty.

Isaiah 54:17 –

No weapon that is formed against thee shall prosper; and every tongue that shall rise against thee in judgment thou shalt condemn. This is the heritage of the servants of the Lord, and their righteousness is of me, saith the Lord.

Isaiah 55:11 –

So shall my word be that goeth forth out of my mouth: it shall not return unto me void [empty*], but it shall accomplish that which I please, and it shall prosper in the thing whereto I sent it.

* Word in brackets added by author for clarity.

Glossary

Anointment [variation of anoint]: To smear, to put oil on, as in consecrating.

Cloak: A loose, usually sleeveless outer garment; something that covers or conceals.

Connoisseur: One who has expert knowledge and keen discrimination, esp. in the fine arts.

Denounce: Inform against; to condemn strongly.

Deter: To keep or discourage (a person) from doing something through fear, doubt, etc.

Emphatic: Felt or done with emphasis; using emphasis in speaking, etc.

Enterprise: Undertaking, endeavor, affair, business.

Entrepreneur: One who organizes a business undertaking, assuming the risk for the sake of the profit.

Mundane: Of the world; worldly; commonplace; ordinary.

Passivity: The state or quality of being passive; esp., inaction.

Plea: A request; appeal.

Similitude: Likeness; resemblance.

Stride: To walk with long steps.

Strife: Contention; fight or quarrel; struggle.

Sublime [variant of subliminal]: Noble; exalted; inspiring awe or admiration.